The Road to New York

by Gary Miller

illustrated by Stacey Schuett

Scott Foresman
is an imprint of

PEARSON

Glenview, Illinois • Boston, Massachusetts • Chandler, Arizona
Upper Saddle River, New Jersey

Illustrations
Stacey Schuett

Photographs
Every effort has been made to secure permission and provide appropriate credit for photographic material. The publisher deeply regrets any omission and pledges to correct errors called to its attention in subsequent editions.

Unless otherwise acknowledged, all photographs are the property of Pearson Education, Inc.

20 ©Ken Stewart/ZUMA Wire Service/Alamy

ISBN 13: 978-0-328-51368-0
ISBN 10: 0-328-51368-7

8 9 10 V0FL 16 15 14 13

"We won!" Julia exclaimed as she and the other Blazers rushed up to the stage to claim their prize.

Julia couldn't remember a better night in her life, ever. The Blazers had been preparing for more than a year for this summer's Double-Dutch state championships. The competition had lasted three whole days, and it included the best rope-jumpers from across the state. But when the judges announced their decision on Sunday night, the Blazers's hard work had paid off!

As the emcee to the competition handed out the other awards, Julia, Carla, Marcus, Robert, and Suki beamed with pride. Watching from the audience, their parents smiled too. It was a big event—but a bigger one was yet to come.

"As you know, as our state's winners, the Blazers have earned the right to attend the National Double-Dutch Jump-Off in August, which will be held in New York City," the emcee said.

The Blazers all cheered. They had been dreaming of the trip to New York ever since the jumping season began. Julia, the unofficial team captain, could already picture the Blazers jumping rope on stage at Radio City Music Hall, where the national championships would be held. She imagined riding an elevator to the top of the Empire State Building and taking the ferry across New York Harbor to the Statue of Liberty. It seemed too good to be true!

Late the next morning, Julia got a call from the Blazers's coach, Mr. Morse.

"I have bad news," Mr. Morse said. "It turns out that the trip to New York will cost more than we'd thought—probably about $3,000. The team has only $400 in the bank. So, unless we can find a sponsor, we won't be able to go."

Mr. Morse explained that he had already called many local businesses that often supported school activities. They made donations that brought the total up to nearly $1,000. But the Blazers still needed more money—a lot more.

"If only we could get a big company to sponsor the team, we could do it," Mr. Morse said. "But none of the people I've contacted so far seem interested. I'm afraid we may have to call off the trip."

5

Julia hung up the phone and sighed.
She and her teammates had practiced so hard,
and it didn't seem fair that the Blazers should
stop now.

Just as Julia was about to call the rest of
the team, her brother Stuart came down the
hall. He was carrying his video camera. This
wasn't unusual—Stuart was obsessed with
movies. When he wasn't watching them, he was
making them. When he wasn't doing either of
those things, he was making Julia's
life miserable.

"What's the matter with you?" Stuart said sarcastically. "Last night you were a champion, and today you look like you finished in last place."

Julia told Stuart the news.

"We'll never get a big sponsor," she said. "I guess we'll just have to start saving our money—maybe we can qualify for next year's championship."

"Boy, you'd never make it in Hollywood," Stuart said. "Directors have to work like crazy to get funding to make their films. But I guess if you want to surrender, you can."

Video camera in hand, he sauntered out the door.

Julia thought about what Stuart had said. Maybe she was giving up too quickly—and maybe Mr. Morse was too. If they couldn't find a big sponsor, they should be able to fund their trip in some other way.

Julia called Marcus on the phone. Marcus had heard the bad news too.

"I guess we just can't go," Marcus said sadly.

Julia told him to cheer up.

"We still have eight weeks before the finals," she said. "That means eight weeks to earn the money we need. Can you call the other team members and ask them to meet at my house tonight at six o'clock?"

That evening, the Blazers got together at Julia's house. Everyone felt like deflated balloons, but Julia tried to convince them that they could make it to New York if they tried.

"We've worked so hard," Julia said. "It seems silly to give up now."

Carla agreed. "Maybe we can earn the money."

Marcus got a big sheet of paper and a marker to write down what they might do. Soon, the paper was filled with ideas. The team took a vote and decided on two of them—a bake sale and a car wash.

The following Saturday, the Blazers held a bake sale in front of the neighborhood post office. Everyone on the team and all of their best friends brought something different. The table overflowed with cakes, cookies, brownies, muffins, and even a pie.

To attract attention, the Blazers did some Double Dutch tricks. Soon the table was empty. The sale was a great success—until the kids counted the money.

"We made forty-two dollars and fifty cents," Julia said. "It's a lot of money for a bake sale. But at this rate we'll never get to New York!"

They decided to make signs for their next venture the next weekend.

The next Saturday, the Blazers held a car wash in front of the school. It was a great location for a car wash—the custodian hooked up two long hoses, and it was on the corner of two busy streets. Lots of people came by, and most were generous with tips. At the end of the day, Marcus counted the money. The Blazers had made more than they had at the bake sale, but they still had a long way to go. Altogether, they had only earned about one hundred and fifty dollars.

"Well, we gave it our all," Julia said. "I guess we just won't be going to New York."

When Julia got home, she was tired and cranky. Unfortunately, Stuart was there too. He was out in front of their apartment building filming a scene for his latest movie, "Tarantula Men from Mars."

Julia told him about the bake sale and the car wash.

"We still need almost two thousand dollars," she said sadly.

"A bake sale and a car wash?" Stuart laughed. "You're not going to make enough money for a New York trip that way! You need to think big, like the filmmakers in Hollywood."

"I don't care about the filmmakers in Hollywood," Julia said. "This isn't some kind of movie, Stuart. This is real life."

Julia went up to her room and tried to forget all about New York, Double Dutch, and especially Stuart. But she couldn't get Stuart out of her mind.

Why did he always pick on her? Why did he always have to be so negative? And why did he care so much about movies? What good were movies anyway? All that talk about directors and Hollywood was really boring.

Suddenly, Julia sat straight up on her bed. She had an idea. The Blazers might be able to go to New York after all!

That night Julia called the other team members on the phone to discuss her idea. She called Mr. Morse too.

"There is no guarantee it will work, but it's certainly worth a try," Mr. Morse said.

The next afternoon, when Stuart arrived home from a friend's house, Julia was waiting in the kitchen with Marcus.

"Oh, look, it's the two jump-rope geeks," Stuart said.

"You wouldn't call us that if you knew about the job opportunity we have to offer you," Julia replied.

"Yeah, right," Stuart said. He began to walk away.

"It's a job you'll like, and the pay is one hundred and fifty dollars."

Stuart froze in his tracks.

"The Blazers want you to make a short video about us," Julia said. "We'll send it to big companies and ask them to sponsor us."

Stuart had to admit that a promotional video was a great idea. "But a hundred and a half isn't much money for all that work," he said.

"You'll be listed in the credits as the director," Julia said. She paused to let that sink in. "But if you want to give up so easily, I'm sure we can find someone else."

"It's a deal," Stuart said coolly. He turned away to hide his ear-to-ear grin.

Mr. Morse worked out a few short routines that showcased the team's abilities. And the team practiced all week to get ready for the shoot.

On Saturday, the Blazers, their parents, and Mr. Morse gathered at the community center. It was a big job, shooting the team's promotional video. Marcus's dad handled the lights. Julia's mom held the microphone. Stuart ran the video camera and did the directing. And the Blazers did what they did best—Double Dutch.

Mr. Morse led them through their routines. First, Julia and Carla did their speed jumping. Then Marcus, Robert, and Suki performed their best stunts.

"We got some great footage," Stuart said. "But shooting the video is just the first step. Now we need to do some editing."

Stuart worked all weekend to edit the video. He put the scenes together in different sequences. He cut out some parts that didn't fit. He even added some cool hip-hop music.

Julia helped Stuart get the job done. At first, she didn't know anything about editing. But as it turned out, Stuart was a pretty good teacher. By the end of the weekend, Julia was even able to do some editing on her own.

"Hey," Stuart said when they were almost finished. "I think you've got some talent for editing."

"Thanks," Julia said. She and Stuart were actually getting along!

On Monday, Mr. Morse and the Blazers met again at Julia's house to put the videos into padded envelopes. With each video, they included a letter explaining who they were and why they needed money from a sponsor. They sent out twenty packages to twenty different companies.

After a week, the responses started coming in. Most of the companies said that they liked the video and wished the team good luck—but they didn't offer sponsorship. The Blazers grew discouraged. The competition was only a few weeks away, and they were running out of time.

Finally, the next Friday morning, Julia opened an envelope from the SuperSpring Shoe Company. The company agreed to sponsor the Blazers!

Julia called Mr. Morse right away. "We're off to New York!" she shrieked.

As quickly as she could, Julia called the other Blazers. Everyone was thrilled! Then she went to find Stuart. It wasn't hard to find him. He was out in front of their building, as usual, shooting a scene for his newest movie, "Tales from the Werewolf's Tomb."

"Stuart," Julia said. "It worked! We have a sponsor! You're a hero!"

"Of course," Stuart said, putting down his video cam. "But I couldn't have done it without you," he added. He smiled at Julia, and she smiled back.

"But you'd better not just stand around celebrating," Stuart said. "You need to practice if you want to win in New York."

"You'd better get practicing too," said Julia. "Because we can't go to New York without our favorite camera person!"

Jump into Double Dutch!

What is Double Dutch? It's a game of jump rope that can be played by three or more people. Two people swing two jump ropes in a crisscross pattern. Then one or more jumpers leap in.

Between the ropes, jumpers can do all sorts of stunts, from pushups to somersaults. Sometimes they just try to jump as fast as they can—this is called speed jumping.

Dutch settlers in New York City first introduced the game in the 1600s. Traditionally, Double-Dutch jumpers sang rhyming jump-rope songs as they jumped. But today's jumpers often jump to recordings of hip-hop music. People jump Double-Dutch all over the world. But it's most popular in American cities.